Oksana Baiul

RHAPSODY ON ICE

LINDA SHAUGHNESSY

CRESTWOOD HOUSE
Parsippany, New Jersey

For Eleanor Shaughnessy,
who, on top of everything else,
watches skating with me

Acknowledgments
I thank the following people for helping to make this book.

Elise Feeley from Forbes Library and Celia Ann Roberts from Simsbury Public Library.
Barbara McCutcheon and Pat Berry of *Sports Illustrated For Kids Online* and Pat Weber and H. Kermit Jackson of *American Skating World*.
Director and coach Bob Young and the International Skating Center of Connecticut.
Sheila Foley, Lois Yuen, and Barb McCutcheon for special photo assistance.
Sandra Loosemore for her World Wide Web window into the skating world; Vikram, Monica, and Debby for video support; and the rec.sport skating newsgroup.

For sharing their words: *American Skating World*, the *Boston Globe*, the *Hartford Courant*, the *Sporting News, Maclean's* magazine, *People* magazine, *Sports Illustrated For Kids, Sports Illustrated For Kids Online*, Barb McCutcheon, and the following sources for specific quotes.
Page 52, *Blades On Ice*, Jan/Feb 1996, "The Gold Championships," Pat and Dorothy Knoell.
Page 8, quotes courtesy of *seventeen* magazine and Susan Swimmer, writer.
Pages 11, 14, 33, *Time* ©1994 Time Inc. Reprinted by permission.
Page 36, *Life* magazine ©1994 Time Inc. Reprinted with permission.
Page 57, Ross Atkin ©1995 *The Christian Science Monitor*.
Page 17, Copyright ©1993 by The New York Times Company. Reprinted by permission.
Pages 16, 20, 26, 29, 31, quotes are reprinted courtesy of SPORTS ILLUSTRATED from the 3/22/93 and 2/7/94 issues. Copyright ©1993 Time Inc. "Teen Ice Queen" by E.M. Swift; ©1994 Time Inc. "Window on the World" by E.M. Swift. All rights reserved.

Carol Weis, Elaine Streeter, Nancy S. Carpenter, and the Hatfield writing group.
Peter, Brian and Keely, Eleanor, and Mom and Dad, who have endured and assisted, each in his or her own way.

Photo Credits
Front cover: Allsport/Anton Want: *t.l.* The Hartford Courant/Brad Clift: *t.r.* Barb McCutcheon: *b.*

Allsport/Anton Want: 21. AP/Wide World Photos: 24, 35, 41, 50; Greg Gibson: 43; Pavel Horejsd: 25; Denis Paquin: 15. The Boston Globe/Tom Herde: 47. Sheila Foley: 31. The Hartford Courant/Brad Clift: 4; Stephen Dunn: 45; Michael McAndrews: 56. Barb McCutcheon: 18, 34, 37, 40, 53, 54, 59. Photoreporters, Inc.: 6. Lois Yuen: 9, 27, 52. Glossary Illustrations: © 1998 David Uhl Studios; Ice Backgrounds © 1998 Bruce Bennet Studios

Library of Congress Cataloging-in-Publication Data
Shaughnessy, Linda.
    Oksana Biaul: rhapsody on ice/by Linda Shaughnessy.—1st ed.
        p. cm.—(Figure skaters)
        Includes bibliographical references (p.) and index.

    Summary: A biography of the young Ukrainian figure skater who won a gold medal at the 1994 Winter Olympics.

        ISBN 0-382-39448-8 (lsb). — ISBN 0-382-39449-6 (scr)
        1. Baiul, Oksana, 1977 or -8—Juvenile literature.
    2. Skaters—Ukraine—Biography—Juvenile literature.
        [1. Baiul, Oksana 1977 or -8 2. Ice skaters.
    3. Women—Biography.] I. Title. II. Series.
GV850.B35S53 1998
796.322'092—dc20
[B]   96-25083

Published by Crestwood House
A Division of Simon & Schuster
299 Jefferson Road, Parsippany, NJ 07054

First Edition
Printed in the United States of America
10 9 8 7 6 5 4 3 2 1

CONTENTS

Like a whirling ribbon, Oksana spins in the spotlight at Hot and Gold.

1

THE UKRAINIAN SWAN

*It is because I have lived a most difficult
life that I could do this.*

• Oksana Baiul (bye YOOL)

"Ladies and gentlemen, Oksana Baiul!"

A spotlight split the dark. At its bottom a 17-year-old girl in a silvery costume posed on the ice, her cheek hot against the stinging cold. As the applause faded, violin music rose around her, coaxing her up into a glide. On flashing feet she swept away.

Beyond the spotlight everything was dark except the tiny lights that circled the ice. But she could feel the eyes of the audience following her. For an instant she was a soaring, swirling blur that set down precariously on one blade. With her hand she picked one foot up high, spun around, and then gently placed it back on the ice. A moment later she stopped still, took a single exquisite step on one toe, lingered, and flitted away. The tenderness of the music was reflected on her face.

At the World Championships in 1993, Oksana mesmerizes audiences with her expressive presentation.

At last she settled back on the ice like a swan on a still pond. The spell broken, the crowd rose to their feet, clapping until their hands hurt. With a huge smile, Oksana stood, bent low on one knee, and bowed.

The event was Hot and Gold, the gala opening of the International Skating Center of Connecticut in March of 1995. As the reigning Olympic gold medalist in ladies' figure skating, Oksana was one of the headliners in what was now her hometown.

Two years had passed since she stunned the skating world by winning the **World Championships.** One writer called it "the once-in-a-lifetime emergence of a super-nova." Oksana had skated onto the ice then as an unknown wisp of a girl from Ukraine (yoo KRAYN). Seconds into her program, she was transformed into a performer with the expression of an artist and the grace of a woman.

Usually skaters, like singers and dancers, develop that kind of ability in their twenties or thirties. Where did it come from in a 15-year-old? Did she learn it from growing up as an only child in the company of adults—her mother, her grandparents, and her coach?

Or did she have this ability because, by the time she was 14, those adults had all left her? Homeless, she had had to fend for herself, cooking on a hot plate and sleeping on a cot in the basement of a rink. All she had had left was skating.

Skating was more than something Oksana Baiul was good at. It was more than a dream. It was her lifeline, her heart, her soul.

2

GRANDFATHER'S SKATES

*From the beginning it felt very natural to me. I liked
the feeling of spinning on the ice, just gliding along.*

• Oksana

On a vast grassy plain in southeastern Europe, just west
of Russia, is a country called Ukraine, meaning "borderland."
Long ago this land was fought over by Mongols and
Tartars, Cossacks and Russian czars. It was part of the
communist Union of Soviet Socialist Republics when
Oksana Baiul was born there on November 16, 1977, in the
city of Dnepropetrovsk (dihn yeh prohp yeh TRAWFSK).
Dnepropetrovsk was closed to non-Communists because parts
for nuclear missiles were secretly made there.

Oksana's father, Sergei (SAIR gay) Baiul, left the family
when she was about two years old. Oksana's mother, Marina,
taught French to earn money for them to live. Marina's
parents lived with them and watched over their blonde
granddaughter with the blue-green eyes, telling her stories.

One of Oksana's favorites was the tale of the Nutcracker. They took her to see it performed, and Oksana wished that she could be in it someday.

When Oksana was three, her mother decided that for fun and fitness Oksana should take dancing lessons. The ballet instructors, how-ever, said she was too young and plump. So her grandfather brought home a pair of skates.

Marina remembered that when Oksana first went to the rink, she stayed on her feet while the other beginners fell. Oksana liked the feeling of moving on ice. Eager to learn, she was soon inching backward and stepping around curves, one foot over the other. She hopped into the air, scram-bling back to her feet when she fell. Neither fear nor bruises kept her from trying again.

One of Ukraine's fine coaches, Stanislav Korytek (KOR uh tek), noticed her while he worked with others at the rink. Though Oksana was only five, he asked her

Oksana plays Clara in Nutcracker on Ice— a wish come true.

9

family if he could teach her and see how far her talent and daring could take her.

Marina Baiul knew that the cost of his coaching, time on the ice, and skates and costumes was more than she could afford on her teaching salary. Also, she didn't want her daughter to miss any school.

The coach explained that the Soviet government would pay for most of Oksana's training and that it had special schools for athletes. Marina Baiul consented, and soon Oksana was on the ice early every morning. She learned how to do single **jumps** and then double ones, spinning twice around in the air.

The Soviet Union had a tradition of great Olympic **pairs skaters** and **ice dancers**. But no Soviet woman had ever won the gold medal for singles skating. It was the dream of many girls, including Oksana.

When Oksana turned seven, her mother said she was finally old enough to go to ballet school. She was also old enough for her first skating competition. According to the movie about her life, *A Promise Kept: The Oksana Baiul Story*, she wore a costume sewn by her mother. Oksana worried that people would laugh at her if she fell. But they didn't. She enjoyed skating for them. And she won!

Oksana decided that ballet school would have to wait. She was going to be a figure skater.

3

NIGHTMARES

My mother will never leave me. . . .
She will always stay in my heart.
• Oksana, to *Time* magazine

In 1986, when Oksana was eight, a nuclear power generator in the Ukrainian town of Chernobyl went out of control. Escaping radiation sickened many people. Radioactive materials fell on the fields of grain that fed most of the Soviet Union. Life, never easy in Ukraine, became more of a struggle. It was soon to become more difficult for Oksana, too.

When she was ten, her grandfather died. Within a year her grandmother also passed away. Oksana and her mother came home each day to an apartment that echoed with memories. They held each other tightly and went on with life.

Skating was not as new and exciting as before. Oksana worked hard, adding other triple jumps to the triple **toe loop** she had just learned. One day she told her mother that she didn't want to skate any more. Encouraging her daughter to solve her own problems, Marina Baiul let Oksana decide what to do.

Oksana quit skating. " . . . for two weeks I felt like a normal girl," she later told *Sports Illustrated For Kids Online* magazine. "I went to school. I slept late. I went out with my friends. I ate what I wanted to eat. And then after a couple of weeks, I felt like my heart was breaking.

"I lost something very important to me. Something that I liked more than my life."

Oksana returned to the rink with new determination. She was competing against girls from all over Ukraine and farther. They could do triple jumps, too.

For competitions, Oksana prepared two programs. One was the **short program**, also called the technical program. It was about two minutes long and included the required jumps, **spins**, and footwork. The other was the **long program**, or freestyle program, which had about four minutes of everything that she could do best. She was also tested on her figures—patterns of **loops** and curls that she traced on the ice with certain **edges** of her skate blades.

The 1988 Olympic Games were in Calgary, Canada. On television, Oksana watched Brian Boitano of the United States and Katarina Witt of Germany win gold medals for figure skating. More than ever Oksana wanted to stand where they were standing—at the top of the podium.

Oksana worked for perfection, pointing her toe out on her **spirals**. Her spins centered on one spot instead of tracing loops like a telephone cord across the ice. Her jumps were high and covered a great distance. She tried to land cleanly on one foot, with her upper body straight.

Her smile, already perfect, warmed the chilly rinks and melted the hearts of those who watched. She liked having an audience, even if it was just the driver of the big Zamboni machine that swept up the ice crumbs and watered the surface.

In 1990, Jill Trenary of the United States won the World Figure Skating Championships. Her movements were feminine, not all jumps and gymnastics. Oksana decided that for women that was how figure skating was meant to be. She was discovering her own style, the artistic side of her skating.

In 1991 she was good enough to compete at USSR **Nationals**. She finished 12th out of all the excellent Soviet skaters, a big step closer to her dream. But suddenly she was living a nightmare.

Normally in good health, Marina Baiul fell gravely ill. Having little time left to live, she told her daughter she would always be with her, watching over her. To remind Oksana, her mother gave her the ring that her own mother had worn. At 36 years of age, Marina Baiul died of ovarian cancer.

Coach Korytek went with Oksana to the funeral. Her father was there, too, but she didn't know him. It was the first time he had seen his daughter in 11 years. After the funeral she went to the rink, brokenhearted. "She was just out there gliding and crying, crying and gliding," said Korytek.

Because apartments were scarce in Ukraine at that time, Oksana had to move out to make room for another family. She left many of her things behind, including her broken clock. Dropping by the apartment soon afterward, she noticed that her clock was working again. In that apparent miracle she sensed her mother's presence.

Oksana stayed mostly with her coach and his wife but had no place to call home. In 1992, Ukraine too was on its own. The Soviet Union broke up into 15 separate countries. When Ukrainian skater Viktor Petrenko won the gold medal at the 1992 Olympics in Albertville, France, he represented the Unified Team, athletes of the newly independent countries.

Though Ukrainians were happy to be free, they struggled with many severe economic changes. They stood for hours in long lines to buy the little bread and meat available. Jobs were scarce, and so was money.

Coach Korytek's support from the government dwindled. There was little money for his skaters to travel to competitions or to buy skates. It was difficult, if not impossible, for his skaters to pay for ice time or for his coaching services. His

On the ice, Oksana pours out her feelings.

own family had to eat. When a job offer came from a skating club in Toronto, Canada, he felt that he had to take it. But he didn't know how to tell Oksana.

Some accounts say that Coach Korytek left when Oksana was away at a competition. Others say that he contacted another coach about her, or even deposited her on the coach's doorstep.

Oksana later told *Sports Illustrated*, "He just bought a ticket and left. He called afterward to tell me, and I understood . . . everyone wants to eat."

But his move was devastating to Oksana. He was a friend as well as a coach, at a time when she needed both. She was a child, with nobody to love her and help her grow. If she opened her heart to someone else, would they leave her, too?

The rink was all she had left. She slept on a cot in the basement. Somehow schooling went on and her clothes got clean and she ate. Most of the time she was on the ice, skating to live and living to skate.

4

ODESSA

She is only one girl. . . .How much can she cost?
• Viktor Petrenko, to *The New York Times*

Ukrainian Viktor Petrenko brought his Olympic gold medal home to Odessa, a handsome city on the Black Sea. He had trained there since he was ten with renowned coach Galina Zmievskaya (gah LEE nuh zihm YEV skye uh). Viktor was engaged to Galina's older daughter, Nina, a ballerina. They planned to be married that summer.

Victor had heard about a girl, Oksana Baiul, who could skate fast and jump high. When he went to watch her one day, he saw more than that. He liked her bright face and her determination. At her level, skaters need new skates every nine months or so. Yet Oksana worked every day in a four-year-old pair that were taped together.

"I did not know it then," Viktor told a reporter for the Boston Globe, "but Oksana had nothing for skating but

Viktor Petrenko and Oksana, the newest members of Galina Zmievskaya's family, play together on the ice.

nothing in her life too." He talked with Galina Zmievskaya. He offered to provide skates for Oksana and donate his leftover fabric for her costumes. Could Galina help, too?

"It was just beginning, you know, her life, and we just wanted to help," said Viktor.

Upon hearing Oksana's story, Galina Zmievskaya felt chills. Galina knew the answer wasn't as simple as taking on a new student. She could not bring Oksana to Odessa without giving her a place to live, and she could not bring Oksana into her home without caring for her as her real daughter.

But Galina already had two daughters, a husband, a mother, a dog, and a cockatoo in their three-room apartment on the eighth floor. When Nina married and moved out, it would still be crowded. Galina's husband was president of a shipping and construction company, but times were hard. Even with Viktor's help, could she afford to raise another child and train another skater? She decided to try.

It was not a simple matter for Oksana either. Galina Zmievskaya was a famous coach. And Oksana had never had sisters or brothers. But Galina had a kind face and a ready laugh. Oksana accepted her offer. With her skates and her mother's ring, Oksana crossed the 250 miles to Odessa and a new life.

The coach's family welcomed Oksana. She moved into a room with 12-year-old Galya, with their beds footboard to footboard. They decorated the walls with needlepoint pictures that Oksana had made. Oksana went to church with Galina's mother. The older woman let the girls practice putting makeup on her as well as on themselves.

The girls discovered that they both loved teddy bears and chocolate bars. They danced wildly to rap music. The cockatoo screamed "Hello" in Russian when the phone rang and danced to the music, too. The people in the apartment below did their own rapping—on their ceiling to stop the noise. It was a merry place. It was a home.

At the Odessa Sports Palace, the two Zambonis were broken. The toilets had no seats. The ice had hills and valleys and algae growing in it, and the edges were dangerously rough. The situation grew worse every day. "No Olympic champion has ever trained in such bad conditions," said Galina Zmievskaya.

Oksana and her coach had to get to know each other on the ice in a different way than at home. Galina had her own ideas about style and tried to teach Oksana how to be beautiful on the ice. Things of beauty, like flowers or stars, may not be perfect or strong, but they have the power to change hearts.

Ballet lessons helped. Naturally flexible, Oksana learned to position every part of her body, right down to her fingertips. She connected her movements so that they expressed meaning and feeling. Back at the rink, Galina helped Oksana combine the elements of ballet with the speed and flow of skating.

The coach was pleased. "It's all natural to her, all God-given talent," she told *Sports Illustrated* magazine. "You tell her something, and she goes, 'Like this?' She does it all on her own."

In December, 15-year-old Oksana competed at the Ukrainian National Championships. She performed a technical program to flamenco music in a sassy black costume and a freestyle program to a medley of songs from Broadway musicals. She won first place—and a chance to represent Ukraine at the 1993 European Championships in January.

At the Europeans in Helsinki, Finland, no one paid much attention to Oksana before the competition. Most of the skaters there had come up through junior international competitions. Judges and audiences knew their names. Few had heard of Oksana Baiul.

Early in her flamenco program, Oksana had planned a

triple **lutz**/double toe loop jump combination. She came down after two spins of the lutz and crashed into the boards in the corner. Getting up, she found that her left skate lace was broken. The referee allowed her to start over, and with a new lace she skated smoothly through the program.

Toward the end of her freestyle program, she had some trouble with jumps. But four good triples and her natural presence on the ice won over the crowd. Who is she, they wondered, as they applauded wildly. The judges liked her, too. France's Surya Bonaly won the gold medal, and the silver medal went to Oksana. Now Oksana was the second best in all of Europe.

Viktor was astounded. He had battled for eight years at the elite level before winning a gold medal. This impish 15-year-old struck silver on her first try. He was very proud of her. Her happiness made him happy.

Oksana's second-place finish meant that she could compete against the best in the world at the World Championships a few weeks away. It was as if she were on a runaway train. It was the ride of a lifetime, but she had to keep working hard if she wanted to go the whole distance.

In her flamenco program, Oksana demands that people watch her.

5

ON TOP OF
THE WORLD

Why does everyone like to watch Oksana Baiul?
Because she does not just skate on ice—she is dancing!
• the Protopopovs, champion pairs skaters

In March 1993 the best figure skaters in the world gathered in Prague, the capital of the Czech Republic. Reporters aimed microphones and cameras at American Nancy Kerrigan. She had placed second and third in the past two years and was expected to win the gold medal this time.

Surya Bonaly, one of the few women ever to attempt **quadruple jumps**, was a strong contender. Lu Chen was a consistent and capable skater from China, where skating was not a popular sport. Again, few noticed Oksana Baiul.

It was difficult for Oksana to focus on practice. There were many skaters there that she had watched and admired on TV, including Katarina Witt. Speaking only Ukrainian and Russian, Oksana had to find another way to communicate with people. She gave her idol, Jill Trenary, a hug.

Oksana was using skates that had crooked blades. Viktor had found her a better pair, but there was not enough time to get used to them before performing. Then, in practice, Oksana crashed into the board wall that edged the rink. When she got up, her back hurt.

A Czech doctor said that Oksana had damaged some disks, cushions of fibrous tissue between the bones that make up the backbone. She had treatments to help her back heal. From then on, she practiced apart from the others. It was painful to skate, but the thought that she might not compete hurt more.

When they called her name in Sports Hall on the night of the technical program, Oksana stepped onto the ice. She had had a warm-up, but still her skates felt strange, not ready to begin. She stroked back and forth at the edge of the rink, breathing deeply. The attention of the audience was on her. Is something wrong? they whispered. What is she waiting for?

At last her skates felt ready. She glided to center ice, made the sign of the cross for God's blessing, and posed.

Her flamenco program was dazzling. Her long legs were as frisky as a colt's. Her arms fluttered like cream-colored ribbons. She soared and spun, and her smile blazed.

Nancy Kerrigan was in first place after the short program. Oksana was second, followed by Surya Bonaly. Oksana and

Oksana flies through her long program at the 1993 World Championships.

others were amazed—she was in a good position to win a medal for Ukraine.

During the freestyle competition two nights later, Oksana stepped onto the ice in a bright blue costume sparkling with sequins. She paused again, increasing the spectators' anticipation, before she went to center ice. A stream of music floated over the rink, and she melted into its flow. Her five triple jumps were high, though she left out the combinations she had planned—one jump followed by another with no steps between. Toward the end of the four minutes, her muscles burned. Her energy was nearly gone. She pushed on until the last chord. Bowing, she left the ice for the next performer.

Surya Bonaly whipped and whirled about, landing seven triple jumps. The leader, Nancy Kerrigan, swept out to music from Beauty and the Beast. While landing a triple **flip** 27 seconds into her program, Nancy's hand grazed the ice.

24

From that moment her performance buckled. She singled or doubled her triple lutzes and **salchows**. When the four minutes were over, she sat in ninth place for the long program and fifth overall.

Lu Chen took the third-place bronze medal. Surya Bonaly came in second. Despite her injured back, Oksana Baiul had won the gold medal. She was the world champion.

1993 World Championship medalists: (left to right) Surya Bonaly (silver), Oksana Baiul (gold), and Lu Chen (bronze)

She cried, from joy and pain. "My tears are God's kisses from my mother in heaven," she told reporters. She was the youngest world champion since 14-year-old Sonja Henie from Norway had won in 1927. Now everyone knew Oksana's name, and they wanted to know her story. They asked about her mother again and again, bringing floods of tears, until Galina asked them to stop.

Oksana returned to Ukraine with the honor and pressure of being the best in the world. Nancy Kerrigan went home to Massachusetts to figure out what went wrong. The two skaters—so exceptional, so different—would soon meet again.

6

BETTER TO
LAUGH

*I like when people are watching. What's the reason
for figure skating without spectators watching?*
• O k s a n a , to *Sports Illustrated*

After winning in Prague, Oksana was invited to be part of
the 1993 Campbell's Soups Tour of World Figure Skating
Champions. She went to the United States for the first
time. For the next two and a half months, Oksana skated in
about 40 cities, along with Viktor Petrenko, Jill Trenary,
Nancy Kerrigan, Tonya Harding, Brian Boitano, and many
other skating legends.

At 15, Oksana was the youngest performer. Viktor
watched over her like a big brother and translated English
into Russian and Ukrainian for her. Brian Boitano and Jill
Trenary, whom she had admired since she was ten, became
her friends. Jill gave Oksana a stuffed rabbit, which became
one of her most prized possessions.

The performers were treated royally, staying in luxurious

hotels and eating fabulous food. Oksana was like a "kid in a candy store," according to Canadian pairs champion Lloyd Eisler. Most of all she loved doing the shows.

Skating could be boring. Sometimes Galina offered Oksana new sneakers or other rewards to entice her to practice. But when Oksana performed, something magical happened between her and the audience. She was like a spark kindling a warm fire.

"She needs an audience," Galina told *People* magazine. "The emotions of an actor are her gift."

Between performing and traveling, Oksana whisked through malls, delighted to sample and purchase makeups and perfumes. She found teddy bears to add to her collection. Joke toys, like fake splattering eggs, made her roar with laughter.

After the tour, Oksana and Viktor returned to Odessa for

On her first Tour of World Figure Skating Champions, Oksana's star quality shines.

serious training. The 1994 Olympic Games in Lillehammer, Norway, were seven months away. The International Skating Union, which makes the rules for world and Olympic competitions, had decided to allow professional skaters to return to amateur status and compete in the Olympics. Viktor chose to take advantage of this decision. So did Brian Boitano and Katarina Witt. Oksana had looked up to them from afar. Now they would be Olympians together.

With his own money, Viktor bought a skate-sharpening machine to use at the rink. On the deteriorating ice in Odessa he, Oksana, and Galina shoveled together, skated together, and laughed together. Ukrainians have a saying, "Better to laugh!" to make hard times bearable.

Galina told a reporter about some special joys of Ukrainians, such as actually getting hot water instead of cold from the hot-water faucet. Sausages tasted incredibly good after people elbowed through crowds and waited hours in line to buy them. It was a treat to skate in other places instead of the mushy mess at their rink in Odessa. They took nothing for granted.

It might have seemed bizarre for Oksana to go from luxury hotels on tour to a housing project between a prison and a cemetery in Odessa. But it was home. She and Galya danced to the songs of Michael Jackson and Madonna. They decorated their room with stuffed animals from fans. Oksana did her schoolwork and continued ballet lessons. And, except for a daily TV break at 10:00 a.m. to watch her Mexican soap opera, she was on the ice.

Several hours a day under Galina's sharp eyes, Oksana fine-tuned techniques such as using deep, clean edges, making good body lines, and staying straight in the air. The Russian pairs champions, the Protopopovs, said that technique was like the roots of an apple tree. Without roots the tree cannot produce fragrant, juicy fruit. Without good technique a skater cannot produce a gold-medal performance.

Oksana vaulted into the air again and again. The **combination jumps** that she had left out at Worlds had to be strong for the Olympics.

"Faster, faster," Galina would call in Russian. "You're jumping like a grasshopper" or "You're acting like a dead chicken."

Oksana would round the end of the rink to try again, her laughter trailing behind her.

7

WORKING ON WINGS

One shouldn't be afraid to lose....this is sport.
• Oksana, to *People* magazine

In the autumn, Oksana decided to make a new short program to the music of *Swan Lake* by Tchaikovsky, her mother's favorite. Like the ugly duckling, she had had a woeful childhood. Now it was time to be a swan.

It was risky to create and learn a new program with the Olympics coming so soon. But Galina, knowing that the new program was important to Oksana, set to work creating the choreography and designing the costume.

The autumn was studded with international competitions, starting with Skate America in Dallas, Texas. Oksana's main challengers were Tonya Harding of the United States and Surya Bonaly of France. Some people questioned whether Oksana was a one-time wonder or a lasting champion.

Oksana told reporters that she didn't need to win all the time. Her goals were to show what she could do and to please the spectators. But Skate America was not a good showing of her skills. In her technical program she left out her triple combination. In the freestyle program she fell on a triple flip and a triple salchow. After missing a jump, Oksana found it hard to be confident about the next one, to remember the hundreds of jumps she had done well in practice. Again, she left out her combinations but held the rest of the performance together, impressing the audience with her maturity.

Tonya Harding's skate blade came loose during one of her performances, and Surya Bonaly had difficulty with her jumps. Again Oksana took first place. However, this win didn't convince people that she belonged where she was.

Viktor Petrenko told *Sports Illustrated*, ". . . she's just starting to understand. The hardest thing is to be the star. Everybody looks at Oksana as the champion, and the champion doesn't have the right to make a mistake."

Though she prefers performing for an audience, Oksana gives 100 percent in a practice for the 1993 Skate America competition.

The champion was growing. At 95 pounds and 5 feet 3 inches, she was two inches taller than she had been the year before. She had more height and weight to center and balance, to whip into the air and land with apparent lightness and ease.

Late in the fall at the Nation's Cup competition in Germany, Oksana came in second, behind German Tanja Szewczenko. At the European Championships in early 1994, Oksana landed five triples but still no combination jumps. Surya Bonaly won with seven triples, and Oksana again came in second.

Meanwhile Nancy Kerrigan had won Pirouetten, a pre-Olympic event in Norway. She was expected to win the United States Nationals and go to the Olympics as the number one American female skater. But after a practice for the United States Nationals in Detroit, she was clubbed above the right knee by an attacker later linked to Tonya Harding. With the shock and sympathy of the world on her side, Nancy worked hard to repair her damaged leg in time for the Olympics.

When both Harding and Kerrigan ended up going to Lillehammer, the attention and pressure were on them. No one bothered Oksana as she prepared for what she had to do.

8

CRASH
LANDING

The bizarre accident not only (created) a new victim but prepared the way for a new heroine.
• Martha Duffy, *Time* magazine

On a Wednesday night in February, 6,000 spectators in the Olympic Amphitheater and a worldwide TV audience watched the first part of the ladies' competition, the technical, or short, programs.

Skating early, Tonya Harding seemed to fall apart under the strain of the past month, finishing 10th among the 27 competitors. Surya Bonaly's performance was show-stopping. Soon afterward it was Oksana's turn. In a feathered headpiece she conjured up a vision of a black swan—her neck bobbing, her arms beating the air. She landed her jumps to much applause. Although she touched an extra foot down on her triple lutz, one expert said it was the best technical program he had ever seen.

Nancy Kerrigan, with a triple lutz, double **axel** and two

Oksana gets last-minute advice before beginning her technical program at the 1994 Olympics.

triple combinations, received the highest marks from seven of the nine judges. As the evening came to an end, the standings were Kerrigan first, followed by Baiul, Bonaly, Chen, Szewczenko, and Witt.

The next afternoon Oksana and Galina went to the rink. For the first time the six leading women were practicing together instead of with skaters from their own countries. Oksana gathered speed with backward crossovers and began the long glide backward into the corner for a triple lutz. At the last minute she saw Tanja Szewczenko about to leap into the same spot. Oksana lunged to avoid her. Szewczenko lunged, too, in the same direction. There was a sickening smash.

Katarina Witt said that it was one of the worst crashes she had ever seen. In shock, Oksana let Witt help her up and then limped from the ice while Katarina went to help her teammate. There was pain in Oksana's leg, and blood trickled out. She had spiked her right shin with her other skate. Her back hurt. Not again, she thought. Not now. She felt as if her life were over.

A Norwegian doctor put three stitches in the cut on her shin, but her back problem was harder to diagnose. The doctor guessed that in the morning it would probably hurt more. He told Oksana to keep ice on it and rest.

Szewczenko's injuries were less severe. She would be able to skate in the ladies' freestyle program the next night. Would Oksana be ready?

Oksana, with coaches Nicolaj Valentin and Galina Zmievskaya, shows her joy as the scores for the short program are posted.

In the morning the pain was still there. Determined, Oksana joined the other girls at practice. There was 24-year-old Nancy Kerrigan, defying the ghosts of her nightmare performance at Worlds and her violent injury. Twenty-year-old Surya Bonaly was reeling off triples like a human whirligig. Oksana felt the pain in her back, and in her heart, as she thought of her chance for a medal slipping away. She had worked so hard. It was a lot for the motherless sixteen-year-old to bear.

She left the ice before practice was over. Some said they saw tears on her cheeks.

9

TWENTY SECONDS

God gives many performers physical talent.
He usually forgets to give them the soul of an artist.
He gave Oksana everything.

• Galina Zmievskaya, to *Life* magazine

As the hour for the start of the long program drew near, Oksana realized that she had no choice. She was in second place. She had skated in pain at the World Championships and had won. She had to skate now.

The Olympic Committee, on the watch for athletes misusing drugs, allowed Oksana to have two injections an hour before the freestyle competition to lessen the pain in her back and leg.

Her long program, to a medley of show tunes, was the same one she had used the year before. Her pink costume was new, handstitched by Galina's mother. It was trimmed with fur and glistened with crystal dewdrops. She wore the ring her mother had given her. She felt Marina watching over her like a guardian angel.

*Refusing to bow to pain and injury,
Oksana goes for the gold.*

Viktor reminded Oksana that she already knew what to do. She just had to go out and do it. They didn't talk about her pain. He and Galina went out to watch the performances, and Oksana waited alone, focusing on her program and praying. She was to be the last of 24 women to compete.

This Olympic ladies' figure skating final turned out to be the sixth most popular event ever broadcast on television. In the final score the freestyle program would count twice as much as the technical one, so any one of the top-ranked competitors had a chance to win the gold medal.

Tonya Harding came hobbling out almost two minutes after her name was announced, trying to repair a broken skate lace. She began her program and stopped, afraid that she would injure herself. The referee said that she could skate again later. Canadian Josee Chouinard was then called to the ice before she was expecting to perform and had a hard time. When Harding returned to the ice, she did not do well either. Surya Bonaly had trouble with jumps. In all, among the 24 women skating, there were 25 falls. Lu Chen pulled ahead in the standings. Two skaters remained.

Early in her program to a medley of Neil Diamond tunes, Nancy Kerrigan had trouble with her triple flip, just as she had in the 1993 Worlds. She pushed on, each movement pure and elegant. She landed five triple jumps, most of them in combination, and a double axel. When the music ended, the crowd went wild. Flowers cascaded from the stands. Most observers believed that she had won, especially after they saw her scores. In the broadcast booth, Olympic champion Scott Hamilton commented that though they were great marks, the judges had left a little opening for Oksana.

Oksana waited while all of the bouquets were cleared from the ice. She stroked around the edge of the rink until her skates felt ready. Her back ached. Her shin throbbed. In the middle of the huge field of ice, she blessed herself with trembling fingers. Her eyes looked at nothing, focused, steady. When her music, like an old friend, called to her, Oksana came to life.

Her triple flip was landed on two feet. She left out combination jumps and doubled a triple toe loop. But she landed a triple loop, lutz, and salchow. Her spins were dynamic. In one, while in a **camel** position, she pulled her free foot back around to her head, becoming a swirling ribbon on a stick. Skating not for perfection but for beauty, Oksana flowed as if she were the song itself. "You could turn off the sound and still hear the music," wrote Michael Boo in *American Skating World*.

Oksana knew that she needed more points for technical difficulty. She had one more jump planned—a double axel. Risking everything, she whipped out a triple toe loop, followed by a double axel/double toe loop combination.

It's over. She did it!

When the music stopped, Oksana covered her head. She had done it! She clasped her hands over her heart. Hearing the thundering ovation, she knew she had done it well. But was it enough?

Waves of joy and pain broke over Oksana, making her gasp with sobs. Galina's arms curled around her as they went to the "kiss and cry" area, where the skaters await the judges' marks.

The judges had 20 seconds to determine the winner, not only of the long program but of the gold medal. The Swedish referee said that it was the hardest decision in her 30 years of judging.

Four judges gave highest scores to Nancy Kerrigan. Four gave highest scores to Oksana. The ninth judge gave Oksana higher artistic scores and lower technical scores than Nancy. But their totals were the same. It was a tie.

But for a tie in a freestyle event, the skater with the higher artistic mark wins. The gold medal belonged to Oksana.

Lost in pain and relief, she couldn't believe it at first. Galina assured her that it was true and whisked her away to make her tear-streaked face presentable for the medal ceremony. While officials searched for almost half an hour for the recording of the Ukrainian national anthem, the crowd buzzed about the outcome.

Many people believed that with so many jumps and combinations, Nancy should have won. But Oksana's lutz was higher, said others, and her spins and footwork seemed more difficult. Some said that Oksana's program had been more expressive and exciting. Others insisted that the judges had watched her smile instead of her feet. Scott Hamilton commented that whether the judges had picked Nancy or Oksana, their decision would have been fair.

At last, Oksana stepped between Nancy Kerrigan and Lu Chen to the top of the Olympic podium. She bowed to receive the medal around her neck. As the light blue and yellow flag unfurled, the anthem, "Ukraine Has Not Died" rang out for its newest heroine.

Wearing her mother's ring, the 16-year-old Olympic champion wipes away a tear.

10

THE GOLDEN
TOUCH

She has this age-less look in her face.
• President Bill Clinton

When Oksana stepped from the plane at the airport in Kiev, a border guard hugged her and gave her a bouquet of flowers. Fans crowded around. She was escorted to Marinsky Palace where the Ukrainian president, Leonid Kravchuk, welcomed her. He handed her a check for $15,000 for winning the gold medal. In Ukraine, where the average worker earned only $20 a month, $15,000 was a fortune.

Oksana went to meetings and dinners, and everywhere Ukrainians praised her. She was a bright light, a symbol of hope in their hard lives. But they had heard a rumor that troubled them—that Oksana was leaving Ukraine, moving to the United States. When they asked her if it was true, she said she did not want to move anywhere. Ukraine was her home.

President Kravchuk asked Oksana and Viktor Petrenko to go with him to visit President Clinton in Washington, D.C.

At the White House, in a sleek dark dress and shoes with high heels, Oksana looked older than 16. President Clinton was glad that she had come.

At a dinner with Vice President Gore and members of the State Department, Oksana and Viktor were asked about the rumor. Viktor confirmed that because of poor training conditions in Odessa, he, Oksana, and Galina Zmievskaya would be moving to Connecticut. They would train at a skating center that was to be built there. They would continue to represent Ukraine in competitions.

Before beginning the Tour of Champions in April, they returned to the drafty Odessa rink. The shortages had grown worse. The airport in Odessa could not get enough jet fuel for the planes. Oksana's injured back was treated at a hospital with good doctors but dirty bedsheets and stained mattresses. There were few bandages or needles or medicines.

Oksana and Viktor visit President Clinton in the East Room of the White House.

An X-ray of Oksana's back revealed that she had one less vertebra than most people. Without that little piece of backbone, she was able to bend like Gumby into positions most people could not reach. The X-ray also showed that she had a chipped vertebra, a minor but worrisome injury.

It was expected that Ukraine, with its many farms and factories, would eventually be able to provide better for its people. But Galina Zmievskaya felt that her skaters could not wait. The cost of living and training in the United States had been too expensive for her to consider moving there earlier. But things had changed.

Ukrainian business people had approached Galina after the Olympics. They had said that with Oksana's talent and her smile, she could be a star and earn a lot of money. Accepting their advice, Oksana and Viktor changed agents and became clients of the William Morris Agency of New York.

And on an April day, with flags snapping and the dust of a tobacco field stinging their eyes, Oksana, Galina, Viktor, and his wife, Nina, stood beside an American skating coach named Bob Young. A crowd of 2,000 people had gathered on bulldozed mounds of earth. There was a Ukrainian children's choir in embroidered costumes singing the Ukrainian national anthem. Kolach, a round Ukrainian bread, was passed around. But they were not in Ukraine—they were in Simsbury,

Connecticut. Oksana mixed a handful of soil from her homeland into the dry American earth.

According to the *Hartford Courant*, Young proclaimed that by October there would be a multimillion-dollar skating center on that very spot. "We're bringing the top skaters in the world to Connecticut!" he said.

Oksana whispered, "I'm very happy." Through the translator she graciously told the people that this would be her second home.

It is 4,800 miles from Odessa to Simsbury. Oksana would have to cross more than miles to live in the United States. She would have to meet new people, eat strange foods, and learn new ways of doing things in a language she couldn't speak, read, or write. As she brushed the dirt from her hands, she knew that somehow she would make it. This time her family was coming with her.

Breaking ground in Connecticut with Bob Young, director of the new skating center, Oksana waves to fans and future neighbors.

11

CROSSING OVER

Sporting News: What's the biggest difference
between Ukraine and America?
Oksana: Cheaper sneakers.

The crossing to America had actually begun with a good
deed in 1987, long before Oksana met Viktor and Galina.
American coach Bob Young had brought a figure skating
pair to compete in Odessa. While performing, the girl fell
from a high lift and crashed. Young rushed from the rink
with his unconscious, bleeding skater, desperate to find
the hospital in a unfamiliar city with an unfamiliar language.
He saw young Viktor Petrenko and asked him for help.
Viktor disappeared.

Young found the hospital, but it was crowded and unclean.
He feared that his skater would get sicker rather than better
if he left her there. Then Viktor and Galina Zmievskaya
arrived, their arms full of clean sheets, bandages, and medicine

for Young's skater. They had purchased these supplies in other countries and then stockpiled them at home in case Viktor got hurt.

Young's skater recovered. The seed of friendship sown that day in Odessa blossomed and later came to fruit when Bob Young invited Galina to his new International Skating Center of Connecticut (ISCC). She could coach top-level singles skaters in the most up-to-date facilities. Viktor and Oksana would have safe ice. Nina could do choreography and off-ice ballet coaching. Viktor's brother Vladimir, a Soviet national champion, could also coach.

Oksana stretches at the ISCC rink.

By October of 1994, the ISCC's Olympic-sized rink was open for practice. Oksana settled her stuffed animals into a townhouse in a little village built for the skaters. Viktor, Nina, and Galina Zmievskaya lived next door. They were

47

soon joined by Galina's mother and Galya and the dog. Other skaters, such as Russian world and Olympic pairs champions Ekaterina Gordeeva (gord yeh YAY vuh) and Sergei Grinkov, also came, making one large, close-knit family.

Oksana skated morning and afternoon, four hours a day. Between sessions on the ice, she practiced ballet and modern dance in front of high mirrors in the dance studio. She worked out in the weight and fitness room. There was a cafe at the rink and a shop with clothing and equipment for figure skating and hockey. There was a room with video games to help skaters pass the time or calm their nerves before a performance.

Watching Oksana practice, young skaters were able to see the sweat and falls that went into making her skating look liquid and easy. Afterward, she often signed autographs for them.

Simsbury was a quiet place, especially for a teenager. During leisure time, Oksana looked for mushrooms in the woods, as people did in Ukraine where the weather was similar. She bought groceries in town, enjoying the attention she got when she was recognized. She explored the nearby shopping mall, sitting at cosmetic counters while the ladies gave her new looks and heaped her hands with samples of makeup in return for hugs. She once took television interviewer Barbara Walters to the mall. Walters had chosen Oksana as one of her Ten Most Interesting People of 1994, along with actor Tom Hanks and former president Jimmy Carter.

With her Walkman in hand, Oksana rarely sat still. In the rink lobby, or in the cafe after practice, she made arrangements with new friends about which house or restaurant or movie they were going to that night. She liked fairy-tale musicals like *Beauty and the Beast* and horror movies. She enjoyed cooking, but when eating out, she ordered Caesar salads, unavailable in Ukraine, and salmon or swordfish, leaving plenty of room for dessert.

Even though she was only 16, Oksana had completed high school. She now had a full-time job—skating. She also kept improving her English. From her friends she learned phrases like "What's up, dude?" She wrote letters in Russian to her Ukrainian friends, but she had to learn a new alphabet before she could write in English or read a magazine or a road sign.

Like most teenagers, Oksana wanted her driver's license. At the registry she learned that she would have to take a course; it was the law—even for Olympic gold medalists. When she finished the course, she could come back and take the test in English or in Russian.

Unlike most teenagers, Oksana often shopped and had her hair done in exclusive boutiques and salons in New York. A movie was being made about her life. A clothing designer wanted her to help create and model skating wear. Promoters

Oksana receives an Inspirational Award at the 3rd Annual Jim Thorpe Pro Sports Awards.

wanted her to compete against champions like Nancy Kerrigan, who had turned professional after the Olympics, and Kristi Yamaguchi.

Before coming to Connecticut, Oksana had planned to spend the next three years as an amateur, training for the 1998 Olympics in Nagano, Japan. But in the new professional competitions springing up, she could be more creative in her skating and earn a lot of money. It was tempting.

The year 1998 was far away. Maybe the International Skating Union would let professionals change back to amateur status as they had before the last Olympics. If not, she already had a gold medal.

She decided to take the risk. In October 1994, Oksana retired from amateur skating and turned professional.

12

ARTIST
ON ICE

She defies people not to look!

• Barb McCutcheon, photojournalist

The transition from amateur to professional was not easy. Rules that Oksana had followed since she was seven no longer applied. Amateurs were limited to instrumental music. As a professional, she could skate to vocal songs like Madonna's "La Isla Bonita." She could experiment with new moves instead of spending hours practicing required ones.

Amateurs worked all year on two programs for competition. But TV audiences expected professionals to do a new routine for each show. If Oksana was flying off every week to perform in different places, how could she work on new routines and keep her body in top condition?

A freak injury made Oksana's transition to professional life even more challenging. Practicing for her first competition

At Skates of Gold, a showcase of past and present Olympic gold medalists, Oksana takes her place beside Anett Potzsch, Katarina Witt, Peggy Fleming, and Kristi Yamaguchi.

in Idaho, she posed at the end of her program, and something in her knee gave way. Arthroscopic surgery followed. Doctors inserted a special scope into her knee to clear away loose cartilage.

A week later at another competition, she was awestruck by a visit from Arnold Schwarzenegger. He said he wanted to meet the girl who had had surgery and two days later was skating again.

During her scheduled performances in November, Oksana smashed into the boards while skating for the World Team in Ice Wars. She fell twice in the Gold Championships. Was the cause of her falls her injured knee or lack of practice time to keep her jumps in shape, or the fact that she was still growing? She was at least another inch taller, and at 17, her body was maturing.

She made no excuses. "It's just my problem, weight and size," she told *Blades On Ice* magazine. "I think I can grow through this problem and next year maybe I'll be skating better."

Occasionally Oksana felt tired of it all. But after a few days off, she was glad to get back on the ice. Some said that the attention of the audiences was propelling her. When she shrugged apologetically at the end of a flawed performance, people cheered and clapped all the more.

Fulfilling her childhood wish, she starred with Viktor Petrenko and Brian Boitano in the *Nutcracker on Ice*. Oksana played Clara, a young girl having her first crush. The show toured 17 cities and was televised on New Year's Eve. It was also made into a video.

In tour and exhibition programs and special shows, such as Brian Boitano's *Skating Romance*, Brian Orser's *Rhapsody in Blue*, and Fox television's Rock 'n' Roll competitions, people glimpsed different sides of Oksana. She skated what was inside her, and they were constantly surprised.

It took courage to try new things. Galina designed a program to Arabian music, with Oksana as a harem dancer. The movements were strange and had to be done precisely to look right. The costume was even stranger, with gauzy,

In Brian Orser's show Rhapsody in Blue, *Oksana shows new sides of her personality.*

In Oksana's Arabian program, the movements are quick, and each one has a meaning.

purple pantaloons split down the sides, a spangled bikini top, and a jeweled turban. Sometimes she wore a mouth veil and held a little lamp.

When she started learning the program, it seemed too hard, too strange to her. But after a few weeks of practice and a couple of performances to break it in, she was enchanting audiences. Her presence was so powerful that photographers could not stop snapping photographs of her.

In the spring of 1995, the International Skating Union gave professional skaters another chance to return to amateur status. The ISU also decided to pay prize money to the winners of their international competitions.

The Ukraine Figure Skating Federation expected Oksana to take this opportunity. She could stay home, train hard, and develop new technical skills. After the 1998 Olympics she would have many years left to continue her professional career.

But 1998 still seemed so far away. And April 1, the deadline for Oksana's decision, was rapidly approaching.

SKATING TO LIVE

People have to do what people want to do. You have to be happy.

• O k s a n a B a i u l t o P a t B e r r y,
S p o r t s I l l u s t r a t e d F o r K i d s O n l i n e

April 1 came and went. Oksana remained professional and ineligible for the Olympics. She said that she was still thinking about it and hoped that the ISU would open the door again. But she was busy and happy with her life. It was full of things she couldn't have imagined for herself a few years before in Dnepropetrovsk.

She had her driver's license and a new green Mercedes. She was skating and modeling and had offers to act in movies. Avoiding the complications of having a steady boyfriend, Oksana had many friends, including some of the greatest skaters in the world. She had a family who loved her and would stand by her, come what may.

Oksana had yet to win a major professional competition. The Riders Ladies Skating Championships in the fall of 1995

At a press conference, Bob Young, Oksana, and Galina Zmievskaya talk about the death of fellow skater and friend Sergei Grinkov.

looked like a good possibility. In the first round she finished in first place, qualifying for the finals at the end of November.

But on November 20, a few days after her 18th birthday, there was tragic news. In Lake Placid, preparing for a show, Sergei Grinkov lowered his wife and partner, Ekaterina, from a lift, lay down on the ice, and died of a heart attack. People in the skating world were in shock, especially in Simsbury, where they had often seen Sergei glide around the rink with his three-year-old daughter, Daria, between his knees.

At a press conference a reporter for the *Hartford Courant* heard Oksana wonder out loud, "God, why do you take from me such good people?" The losses in her past were flooding over her. She went to Moscow for the funeral, returning just before the Riders Ladies final in Boston.

Oksana had to skate three programs. Though she had been

away from the ice for ten days, her first performance was brilliant. In the second, she reduced her jumps to singles and doubles, slipping to second place overall.

For her third program she wore a black costume and transparent black shawl. The announcer told the audience that Oksana was dedicating this program to a friend, Sergei Grinkov. Fighting to control her emotions, she began.

She had adapted a program to the song "You'll See" by Madonna. Once again Oksana was ". . . gliding and crying, crying and gliding." She faltered on her jumps, but her movements flowed, from heartbreaking softness to fist-clenching fury and back again, until the last chord faded. In the silence, on her knees, she curled over and wept hot tears onto the ice. Many wept with her.

When the competition was over, Oksana had dropped to fourth place. Some said it was unprofessional to risk her chance of winning by skating an unplanned program. Others said that she should not have skated at all, being in such an emotional state. But people will remember that performance long after they have forgotten who came in first.

"Every competition is important to me." Oksana told the *Christian Science Monitor*. "Skating is my life." However, during the 1996 season, she did withdraw from several competitions. She underwent therapy for her back injury from

Lillehammer and spent little time on the ice. Some say it was her sudden fame and fortune that kept her away—too much too soon for anyone to handle. Only 19, Oksana seemed to need a new dream or goal to aim for.

In early 1997, driving well over the speed limit and under the influence of alcohol, Oksana careened off the road into some trees. She received 12 stitches for a cut on her head and was arrested. In addition to enrolling in an alcohol education program, she arranged to do community service to help others avoid the dangers of drinking and driving.

In her autobiography, *Oksana, My Own Story*, published just before her accident, Oksana wrote that skating will always be part of her life. Her many fans hope that is true. There are other skaters with grace and spirit and style. But no one gives those gifts back to an audience like Oksana Biaul, the harem girl, the Broadway beauty, the swan.

To Oksana, that is what skating is for. That is what life is for.

Oksana's joy for skating and for life triumphs over all.

GLOSSARY

axel

A jump with a forward take-off on the outside edge of one skate, rotation(s), and an extra half-turn to land on the back outside edge of the opposite skate.

camel

A one-foot spin with the body and other leg in a horizontal position.

combination jump

One jump followed by another, with no steps or turns between.

edge

The sharp inside or outside rim of the blade of a skate.

flip

A jump from the back inside edge of the skate, boosted by the toe of the other foot from behind. After rotating, the landing is on the back outside edge of the other skate (the boosting foot).

ice dancer

A skater who, with a partner, performs routines requiring dance elements, almost constant contact, and no lifts above the waist.

jump

Any of the various ways of leaping into a spin in the air and landing. The turns can be single, double, triple, or quadruple.

long program

The second part of a competition, also called the freestyle program, lasting 4 or 4 $\frac{1}{2}$ minutes and showing the skater's best skills and artistry.

loop

A jump taking off backward from an outside edge and landing in a backward direction on the same edge.

lutz

A jump taking off from a long glide backward on the outside edge of one skate, with a boost from behind from the other toe. The backward landing is on the outside edge of the opposite (boosting) skate.

Nationals

The yearly competition held in January or February to determine the champions who will represent a country at the World Championships and Olympics.

pairs skater

One of two partners skating in harmony and performing routines, including spins, jumps, high lifts, and throws.

quadruple jump, quad

A jump with a spin of 4 rotations, or 4 ½ for a quad axel.

salchow (SOU COU)

A jump starting from a back inside edge, landing backward on the outside edge of the opposite skate.

short program

The first part of a competition, also called the technical program, lasting 2 minutes or 2 minutes and 40 seconds, including required moves such as 3 jumps, 3 spins, and 2 sequences of footwork.

spin

A twirling movement in a variety of positions, on either foot or both feet.

spiral

A one foot glide, forward or backward, with the other leg extended back straight and upward.

toe loop

A loop jump, assisted by a boost from behind from the other toe.

World Championships

Competition between national champions to determine the best skaters in the world, usually held in March.

COMPETITION RESULTS

AS AN AMATEUR

Year	Competition	Result
1991	USSR Nationals	12th
1993	Ukrainian Nationals	1st
	European Championships	2nd
	World Championships	1st
	Skate America	1st
	Nations Cup	2nd
1994	European Championships	2nd
	Olympic Winter Games	1st

AS A PROFESSIONAL

Year	Competition	Result
1994	Ice Wars, World Team	2nd
	The Gold Championships	2nd
1995	Ice Wars, World Team	2nd
	The Gold Championships	2nd
	Fox Rock'n'Roll Figure Skating Challenge	1st
	Riders Ladies Skating Championship Series	4th
1996	Fox Rock'n'Roll Figure Skating Challenge	2nd

◆ ◆ ◆

TOURS AND SHOWS

1993, 1994, 1995, 1996	Tom Collins' Campbell's Soups Tour of World Figure Skating Champions
1994, 1995	Nutcracker on Ice
	Skates of Gold
1995	Hot and Gold I and II
	Too Hot to Skate
	Rhapsody in Blue
	Skating Romance
	Wizard of Oz
1996	Tribute to Sergei Grinkov

FOR FURTHER READING

About Skaters

Browning, Kurt, and Neil Stevens. **Kurt: Forcing the Edge**. Toronto: Harper Collins, 1991.

Burakoff, Alexis. **On the Ice**. Newton, MA: Hare & Hatter Books, 1994.

Donahue, Shiobhan. **Kristi Yamaguchi: Artist on Ice**. Minneapolis: Lerner, 1993.

Faulkner, Margaret. **I Skate!** Boston: Little Brown, 1979.

Gordeeva, Ekaterina, and E.M. Swift. **My Sergei: A Love Story**. New York: Warner Books, 1996.

Hilgers, Laura. **Great Skates**. Boston: Little Brown, 1991.

Orser, Brian, and Steve Milton. **Orser: A Skater's Life**. Toronto: Key Porter Books, 1988.

Sanford, William, and Carl Green. **Dorothy Hamill**. Parsippany, NJ: Crestwood House, 1993.

Savage, Jeff. **Kristi Yamaguchi: Pure Gold**. New York: Dillon Press, 1993.

Shaughnessy, Linda. **Elvis Stojko: Skating From the Blade**. Parsippany, NJ: Silver Burdett Press, 1998.

_____.**Michelle Kwan: Skating Like the Wind**. Parsippany, NJ: Silver Burdett Press, 1998.

_____.**Scott Hamilton: Fireworks on Ice**. Parsippany, NJ: Silver Burdett Press, 1998.

About Skating

Indiana-World Skating Academy. **Figure Skating: Sharpen Your Skills**. Indianapolis: Masters Press, 1995.

Milton, Steve. **Skate: 100 Years of Figure Skating**. Toronto: Key Porter Books, 1996.

Sheffield, Robert, and Richard Woodward. **The Ice Skating Book**. New York: Universe Books, 1980.

Smith, Beverley. **Figure Skating: A Celebration**. Toronto: McClelland & Stewart, 1994.

Van Steenwyk, Elizabeth. **Illustrated Skating Dictionary for Young People**. New York: Harvey House, 1979.

Stories About Skating

Dodge, Mary M. **Hans Brinker or the Silver Skates**. Sisters, OR.: Questar, 1993.

Lowell, Melissa. Silver Blades series: **Breaking the Ice** (1993); **Competition** (1994); **Going for the Gold** (1994); **In the Spotlight** (1993). New York: Bantam.

Streatfeild, Noel. **Skating Shoes**. New York: Dell, 1982.

INDEX